T0078390

TO MY
GARDEN

Edward Holman

authorHOUSE

AuthorHouse™
1663 Liberty Drive
Bloomington, IN 47403
www.authorhouse.com
Phone: 833-262-8899

Published by AuthorHouse 12/02/2020

ISBN: 978-1-6655-0824-7 (sc)
ISBN: 978-1-6655-0823-0 (e)

Print information available on the last page.

This book is printed on acid-free paper.

Contents

Dedication

The poem "For You" on page 48 and "the castle"
illustration on page 50 are dedicated to the
singer Bono and the band U2.

The poem entitled "Arches" on page 32 and "the lion and
the lamb" illustration on page 34 are dedicated to
Carl Gustav Jung.

The Angels of Armageddon

When I'm driving in my car I can see
the Angels of Armageddon. I see
the expression on my face in the mirror
and then know that wherever I proceed
there have to be Angels of Armageddon.
Not because where I go doesn't get me to
where I belong yet because the Angels
express their feelings to me.

They are not conning anyone. They stare
right into my eyes and know that
I don't want to be conned.

Remove the darkness from their eyes
Oh Angels of Armageddon! Let those who
still have hardness in their hearts without
fairness of reason, cry! Let them continue
in their rebellious hearts to do whatever
turns your anger into a peaceful calm.
Before you is the storm Oh Angels.

I follow only you Angels of Armageddon!
You finally have become friends to me.
Why should I be frightened of words when
I am a word? Should I be frightened of myself?

I crave to love!
I crave to feel!
I crave emotion!

I crave the earth where I can whisper
sweetly to anyone who doesn't want me
for the parcels that I can give them but want
to sing to me the songs that I have yet to sing.

I crave your touch Oh Angels! And if you
whisper fearsome words then I crave your
instruction and peace.

Oh My Brief Love

Oh my chaste heart. Body unkempt.
Sometimes I see the stars beautiful
and brief in their existence compared
to you
Oh Love.

Oh my chaste soul. Cities about.
Sometimes I see the clouds wet
in their brevity compared
to you.
Oh friend.

Oh my brief longing. Brief wanting.
Brief desire.
Sometimes I see the eyes of my
love busy in their life
without me.

Oh I compare them to the sun.
Shining – Giving light and warmth.
Briefly
Lovingly
Chaste.

Hands

The storm is up. It is my cup.
This work it is my food.

My hands show me they don't
bleed like memories.

I will be my hands.
They were not made to hold
prisoners or construct prisons.

I wash my hands
They hold me and
Breathe for me
They Tend to me
And feed me

My hands are on fire

I will begin to walk on them
again. Then run
and fly.

My hands are lovers praying
for marriage

Fear not hands
Someday you will hold each
other without judgment.

Lovers left alone –
Loving

Fear not hands

Hold me
Breathe for me
Tend to me

Wash me

At Such Times

Words sprawl luxuriously in styrene cities.
Pick up pen. It is nothing. Writes nothing.
Prepares for nothingness.
Glance in the mirror at one decayed.
One tossed his head. Time ago.
Remarkable gesture.

This eye. This face
Free of creativity.

Stench of analysis. Rules and weapons.
Slaughtered forests –
Guidelines for the gifted
dancing with frightened bullets.
Scared guns.
Fearless weapons.
Rules for religious machines
Volunteering in groomed wheelchairs.

One who had really been.
One who had really seen.
How chaste the plastic had become.

They have succumbed. For wanting. Needing.

Straight healthy bones to prop up jaws.
Oh how envious. How gigantic. How moral.

Precise – Pertinent

At such times gather up the dawns who roam.
Make a prophecy, coming home.
Try not to pronoun one to death.
Instead a big noun catching breath.

Soaked in moral sores.

The Linoleum Poem

Everything that is not real is linoleum.
Everything that is real looks like wood.

The boy and the girl next door are wood.
My plants are wood. My feet are yes, yes, yes wood.
Smooth as the surface of a freshly buffed nail
and childhood sweethearts are wood.

This is I know is psycho babble or the babble
of a psycho. Honestly though it surely will snow
and the ground will be unholy sludge. And
lately I know that if I don't let go I'll be
an unholy drudge.

If Mars has some liquid – no one will tell. The
fact is nobody knows. Venus is hotter than a
fresh piece of toast and the boy wearing black
blows his nose. He's crying over a flower he picked.
Did the love me, love me not routine.
Paradise forgotten oh it's a camera with film -
Or a fresh off the rack magazine.

Somewhere in time beautiful refrigerators
hum marvelous, electronic tunes. Harps are
sublime while VCR's whine and microwaves
microwave on the moon.

My very fine and good piece of wood burns
delightfully before me. I believe I won't tell
if it's heaven or hell. I'll roll my linoleum dice
and we'll see.

Pans and plates and fresh coffee brewing, this
is what time is made of. Paper and towels,
curtains, carpet and chair to sit down in when
you've had enough. But tomorrow, oh tomorrow
could be the day all of the madness will end. So I
will eat anyway and I won't be sentimental. No
I won't be sentimental at all.

Did You Hear My Song

Oh God did you hear my song?

What I mean to say is that it wasn't really
my song it belonged to someone else and
I liked it so much I just had to
call it my own

I know I shouldn't have stolen every
word but I knew what they were saying
and I just had to have them

I know I shouldn't have taken every note
but they sounded so good I
whistle them all the time.

Can I at least say it's my song right
now I only really wanted to borrow
it but I promise I will give it back as soon
as I am finished with it or at least until
I find someone else.........

to give it to

The Mansion

A man had a mansion. He also had many servants
who knew all the rules of his house. He made the
rules because he entertained many guests who
visited his great house and had little or no control
if they were not reminded of his rules. His
servants were told to remind his guests should they
get out of hand and do damage to his house. Now
the man's best friend comes to visit him. The friend
truly loves and respects the man but he does not relax
any of his rules for his friend and neither do his
servants. His friend obeys the rules to the best of
his ability. However, each time he is corrected or
needs to be reminded of the rules he feels deeply
hurt because he is not being treated better than
a guest. The friend departs with many feelings to
overcome and think about. Later the owner of the
mansion sits down and ponders this fragile situation.
His guests have gone their merry way and he knows
they were only obeying rules for their own interest
and pleasure, to avoid reminders from his servants
and not to have to leave his beautiful house. The
owner says "I will invite my friend to stay permanently,
for he obeys rules out of love and respect for me."
"I will have those guests in my house no more. They
only obey rules out of selfishness and when they
break them they only pretend to be sorry."

"My friend is truly sorry when he breaks or is reminded of my rules. I will ask him to bring his friends with him to my house because I know I can trust his judgment."

Frog

Frog my lips with don't stop energy

Coming breath is a frog

Stop kissing – Frog is looking
Stop trying – Be the frog

He is not

like some

but he would be if I'm not like
this frog who basks

I am so shut – in time – frog will
grow big

See frog lips jumping

breathing running

Seeing more frogs everyday
for my game

My Frog

Green Clean

My artistic – incomprehensible

frog

The Fly

Oh my! What a beautiful fly! I'm no entomologist but I am just stunned by your loveliness.

Oh no! A fly swatter.

Run Fly Run! Fly! Fly. Fly!

Thy Welcome

The sky told me that I must become more
involved in my endeavors – soon – for the
Winter of my life is at hand and the seeds on
trees descend upon me to remind the earth and
the Author that they must fall and die to be
born again. And nature is not imploring nor
foolish with its desires.

Then the sky informed me and the soul
I was appalled by might yet become a pillar for integrity.
So I reasoned that my guidance
would come from nature. And soon I might
not need the world or its approval.

And departure from the world may be
an imminent friend or foe. I could not be real
enough alone for nature itself insists that
its reality needs our relationship.

So I disrobe for the sky and I
am naked in tears.

Undisguised for thy welcome.

Art is Everywhere

And Art is everywhere now.

Not is some stuffy museum that's closed
on Sunday and opened on Monday. A place
where you need to be quiet and polite and
know who did the work and when. Know
their pretty lives. Their petty lives.

What body part they cut with knives.

It's you and I and we're naked – running
on a carpet of clover. The beautiful, warm
wind touching us gently.

No – More – Shame.

We're painting canvasses with the
fruits and berries that fall off the trees. And
no one is guarding that Vincent van Gogh
painting because it's in a gallery on Mars
that is only a hop, skip and a jump for
beings who fly swiftly through space and
can drink sulfuric acid right out of the cup
without batting an eye.

And Art is everywhere now.

And it is even more beautiful too because
it is worth rescuing and saving like us.
And we're naked – running on
a clover carpet.

No – More – Shame.

And it is more beautiful to forget
than to remember. You forgot about
longevity when you learned to fly.

And I forgot about sorrow when I couldn't
remember how long ago I cried. I got
something and gave something and
finally forgot what the problem was.

Because the market of worldliness fell
on that black day and no one jumped
out of the windows unless they wanted
to laugh directly at the ground that they
swerved to avoid as the sky lifted
them ever upward.

And Art is everywhere now.

And it's so much more beautiful to
forget than to remember.

Brave New world

Oh brave new world dost not
though know? There among the
winds did go, a specter who
marched in dark crusade -
More than any brave parade.

Oh hungry orb that spins
the sun. For all here children
are undone. No mercy would
she show me for mercy that
I gave. Silent and slow who
could perceive – comes the
chaste and quiet blow.

Oh fire sky not one dare say.
How tomorrow brought today.
Though many go on speaking still.
Of the lifetime they will fill.

Oh lone affair has brought the hand,
to hide the eyes of those who stand -
In the way or in the path -
Of paradise and helpless wrath.

I Write the Wind

I write the wind because I cannot
move my legs from where I
stand with you.

I drink the sun because we
have shared this cup
of pain.

I lift the sky and hurl it into the ground.

You see over there the rain.
You see there the hail.

Yes I crawled from the deepest trenches
of darkness to catch a glimpse of you.

I see you now.

Oh but you are a strange bird.
But sing to me. Oh sing to me.

Sing the song of hope.

The song that birds sing when
they wait in a forest tree.

Sing a song to me.
Sing a song of me.

Intone an old hymn or one
that is new.

But Oh please sing for I
need you to.

The Power

Oh I had the power to loosen you once
like a knife to a stuck jar of jelly.
And I had the power to paint by number a
beautiful portrait on your canvas.

Your canvas Dammit!

And I had the power to escort you to just
about any decent play you might want to see.
Or read to you some the crummiest poems you
might ever want to hear aloud.

Aloud Dammit!

I had the power to show you another side
to yourself that I'm sure you missed and
are still missing. But you took the power
away from me.

Dammit

Dammit all to hell!

Pity and Sorrow

Pity and sorrow run for tomorrow.
Pretty we borrow. Lovely we borrow.

Patches of obsession cover the skin.
Beauty we win. Graceful we win.

Love and desire holding them out.
Without a doubt. Holding them out.

Promise and duty afraid to speak.
Strangers I seek. Outsiders I seek.

Bloody and dusty wind sweeps the sky.
Should angels cry? Would angels cry?

Offers to myself and offers to him.
Creme de la crème. Creme de la crème.

Desert and sand. Cups in our hand.
Naked we stand. Defenseless we stand.

Glory and shame, whispers our name.
One and the same. Together the same.

Steps on the moon. No poem or tune.
Over the dune. Under the dune.

Seventeen Questions. One Statement

Did you inspire the sun to be afraid of you?
Or is the sun afraid of you because you are so gentle?
Do you want to be alive in the best moment of your life?
Or dead in the worst moment?
Does your love crucify the desires of your enemy?
Or does your enemy crucify the desires of your love?
Do you want me to pray that things work out right?
Or pray that I may even come to know the meaning of right?
Will the stars fall when they see your face?
Or is your face the mirror of the stars?
Is it honest for me to wish for a dream?
Or honest for you to still be able to share the dream?
Should not a traveler always keep his destination in mind?
Or will his journey lose a part of its importance if he does?
Am I to understand that I am where I am supposed
to be and you are not with me?
Or am I to recognize that I am supposed to be able
to understand that you are with me in spirit?
And in this infinite spiritual love am I just a piece
of decaying flesh and blood imprisoned upon a
doomed planet that has nothing but
a history of death?

Yet even in my relentless struggle for survival with tears
of joy and pain and agony, remorse and sympathy. I
do not blame you and still know that you love
and care for me.

Bridegroom

How perfect and brave you are Oh Love.
My love has nothing to fear.
Through death of a thousand kingdoms.
Their castles disappear.

How sweet the sound of words you say.
My ears delight me so.
The cadence of all drummers, a
thousand bands shall never know.

How many loves have I of you.
All storybooks can't tell.
How many dreams have I of you.
A bottomless wishing well.

How much the wind has softened time
since I discovered you.
A rainbows end on mountains high.
A voice with sounds anew.

How beautiful your garden. The trees
and flowers abloom.
I will rest here forever in tapestries
of your loom.

And I will always speak or your love,

My dearest..........Bridegroom.

The Conscientious Porter

A porter is carrying the baggage of a dignitary to his room. He knows that he will receive ample reward for his prompt attention. On the way a woman stops him to ask for a towel. He doesn't put the bags down but politely informs her where she can get one. After this a man slows him down to ask him for directions to a certain restaurant. "They can tell you that in the lobby around the corner sir." The porter continues on his way. Now a little boy who is lost approaches him. The porter drops the bags and says to the child. "Sit down for a minute." "Your father is surely looking for you." The porter talks to the boy while they are waiting. In a few minutes the child's father turns the corner in the hall, expresses his great joy and gratitude to the porter. Then he takes his son by his hand and leaves. Finally the porter comes to the dignitary's room. The dignitary states in anger. "Do you have any idea what an important man I am?" What took you so long." Sir, an important matter came up along the way," said the porter. "More important than my things," the dignitary angrily replied. "I will have a word with your supervisor. I could have you dismissed from your job for being so slow." "Yes, I know, said the porter. "Where shall I put your baggage?"

The Meaning

Didn't you make me run for the meaning
carrying boxes of tears? Do I know who
I am when I'm alone or do I need the
boxes to remind me?

So I searched for your body and found it
beautiful enough inside of me.

I thought I didn't need you and was sure
I didn't want you as much as I wanted
not to want you.

But I absorbed you against the tide of my
will and felt all the creatures in the
ocean of my being crawl upon the sand
and relinquish themselves.

So there was moisture everywhere.

And I thought that there is or was
nothing warmer than the way
you are inside of me.

So now I run to hear the sound of myself.
Not to leave you with my boxes of tears.,
but to hear the sound of your soul......

singing in me.

Poem 67

I look at words now and see the
vanity of immortality. To think
a mere word will remain on a page
when even I must go to the wind.

The bottom of the ocean seems a proper
resting place for words. They might lie
upon the surface of the water then
slowly become the basin.

I once thought that words could create
such a flame as to burn pages out of the book.
I went digging for them in a place that once
took care of words. I found the silence suitable but a sense of
belonging was missing.

I felt perhaps someday I would become
a word and go to this silent place.
One gets old, wanders then suddenly becoming
a part of the book is not as important as
being free from the sentence or the page.

Being the most valuable word and belonging to the most significant work would still create an urgency to be recognized and a strong dependency on a reader.

The word am can be I.

I will be morning.

Unfinished Thoughts

Unfinished thoughts were about in the air.

It was out there in the desert that I saw
the clouds hanging low.

Darkness congregating, then vanishing.

Gray, gray landscape – Dry as the tongue that
would speak to the sun and cold as
the corridors of the mind.

This place was certainly born here tonight.
The moon says so and the stars refrain.

But it is the ground that listens and waits
for the coming footsteps.

And it is the ground that will
move here tonight.

Oh stars – If I would have known on the
day that I was born I would have
died that day.

Oh moon – It would be fine to be as realistic
as something so very old to shine
like one so young.

Oh ground – I will lie here and wait with you.

Perhaps sleep.
Perhaps dream.

Arches

I once had arches. I was a place to eat,
a gateway bridge.

A foot.........in the door
of those buildings is a man standing.
I can see him.

He looks as if he had had a
gun he would shoot it.
I would not walk to him
without my arches.

Suppose I crawled.

Just suppose for a minute that another
man is standing at the door.
Behind the first man. In front of
him. It doesn't matter. There is
another man there.
I can see him.

Their love for each other is boundless
and timeless. Yet one man is pushing
on the door while the other is pulling.

I saw the two men let go of the door
and embrace, and then I saw so many men
try to get into the building and so many
try to get out.
Some wanted to eat.
Some wanted to stop eating.

I got my arches fixed by a doctor.
Doctor Love.
Doctor God.

He wasn't in the building
where the men were eating. Nor
was he outside waiting for a table.

He was preparing the meals and fixing the arches.

Car World

We live in a car world

A brick world
A glass world

A far world away from me.

We live in a broke dream

A smoke screen

Awake me Oh friend

I can't see.

I wanted to touch you
To hold you
To heal you

But they took you away from me

Maybe I'll wake up
and take up

My courage again someday.

But today it's a car world

A brick world
A glass world

A way to be.

Quotations

Greater than knowledge. Sympathetic tears
and the wings of the butterfly.

❧

The warrior with no weapons is the most
shrewd, having only ingenuity and courage.

❧

Poet: One who churns out much food for
thought to many who give little or no
thought how he gets his food.

❧

The lonely person is not necessarily one that
doesn't keep the company of others. But
the company of others keeps them.

❧

If you spill a lot of milk. Go ahead and cry.

❧

All around is chaos including the minions
who insist they are doing the right thing.

❧

What the many think and say are oceans
compared to a few quiet raindrops, who know.

You Make Me Cry

Oh you make me cry and I don't know
how the stars shine so willingly. The sun
seems to become your face as you lie
on sand in the morning.

The wind carries my thoughts of
fear away when I'm near you. And
the rain gently showers to wash us.

I love the sun the wind and
the rain.........

and you make me cry.

Song of Pleasure

I'm a cell. I'm a video recording. I'm a shell.
Because it pleases him, and may as well.
I was falling but I picked up my feet.
I heard a calling and was afraid to retreat.
So when you open up the metal door and
slam it in my face. It's the only way you
can ignore the fallen human race.

I'm a sin. I'm a supermarket bottle. Pizza tin.
Because it pleases him. So let me win.
I was stalling but I picked up the beat. The
cadence falling. Sure I was brave to repeat.
So when you empty out the silent halls and
put your fears to bed. It's the only way
these teardrops fall down from my lonely head.

I'm a top. I'm a black conveyer belt. A dirty
mop. Because it pleases him. Don't want to stop.
My hands were tied. My knees were on the ground.
Witnesses lied. I didn't make a sound.
So when you pour the filthy bastard smoke
into the filthy sky. It's the only way you'll
ever look the bastard in the eye.

I'm a joke. I'm a civil service test. Don't
count I'm broke. Because it pleases him. Just
watch the smoke. The bed that teases them.

I'm an astrologic piece of an astrologic pie.
Supersonic grease for a supersonic lie.
So if the psychodrama super group should
grasp the truth, get the scoop.

It pleases him. It pleases him. It pleases him.

Haiku

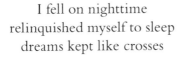

I fell on nighttime
relinquished myself to sleep
dreams kept like crosses

Nothing but green weeds
arise from deserted cracks
in vacant cities

Many tears that fall
upon our seas and landscapes
could hold an answer

Leaves dance down from trees
gather on grass, whispering
Autumn impressions

Eternity knows
those who fill their cups with tears
and unfinished songs

Every planet turns
around the sun as it burns
every son who burns - waits

The Tongue

You want to take it off of the shelf
and rip it to shreds –

Or kiss it –
It's ugly and it's beautiful
at the same time –

It's a boy – It's a girl –
It overpopulates the world

She wants one – He wants one –
We all have one –

It sticks out – It sticks in

And will wipe off that grin –

It's a sin when you win –

Then again –

Amen

Noses

Return the river over the pond.
Creation – Formation

Pond sees quick old sons. Evil neck boxes
lower shoe holes. One box dry. Two crumbs in
my soup cleaner.

Zipper goes up. Bottom in my soup. Flying trees
in boxes where rooms melt tiny bulbs. Fish eyes toward
box. Barracudas melt ships that fly to ponds where
the dog toads run over fish boxes.

Trees in forest mist fall on monkey plates when
hose bricks bark and cry.

Atmosphere – Ionosphere

Come drink the dust in my nose. Love oozes from
my nose. Blood falls from my nose onto table.
Broken books breathe from my nose. Broken
dishes crash in my nose like noses on planets should
respire when they are breathing.

Nostrils suck wind from hair when planets rest
and form snouts to suck in other planets who
in turn hold their noses.

Nose planets inhale solar systems where pungent
aroma songs howl in trees.
Pig frogs bark at toad dogs and a broken
emergency nose howls over an entire moon.
And soon a system of planets acquires its very own
pig to wallow around in its moon song.

Soon all snouts get whatever the moon wants when the
moon blows a tree horn. This wakes the tide with
dog fish swirling in long trees.

Sulking pigs may walk about looking for odors
in noses green but the sun shall walk in plots
full of noses breathing.

Fresh sun walking. Grinning at other suns whose
schnozzes haven't quite been near a tree of frozen frogs.

So without much assistance noses continue to make
history by running to planets and suns whose nostrils
lift up the trees of the moon.

Hard Dream

And it was such a hard dream. But that hard
dream helped me cover the day I was a fool.
And those dreams deliver tears. Who knows where?

So I fixed my eyes upon the battlefield and the
more I conquered the enemy the more I
had to cover the day I was a fool.

And I covered that day with grief.
I covered the battlefield with lamentation. Then
I covered the enemy upon the battlefield
with salt.

It was a sweet season I had been
delivering.

Dreams – They're hard man.
Because you're in them whether you
want to be or not. And
reality. Who knows?
It gives you a whole lifetime of
days to be a fool.

Days you can be sure you want
to be in.

And days covered with salt.

Hated Love

I was small when I fell. Hated love
in pollen. Who didn't hate love?

I grew and fell when I wanted to
love my flesh that I hated.
The flesh that belonged to me and no one else.

Oh was it the hated love of someone else.

I hated knowing that I might touch
you and be eternally satisfied or
never satisfied until I owned the
skin that your blood dripped on.
Owned as one who wouldn't shun ownership.

I grew more and only hated knowing that
if your flesh was separated from your
body and spirit I could not choose which
I wanted more.

I shrank away from love and sank
my teeth into my own flesh and
drank the blood that I own.

Then I hated the thought that it
could taste the same as yours
and not belong to you.

I love your flesh and your blood
and spirit.

And I cannot grow anymore hating to
know that I might have to choose
among the three.

For You

For you some cut down trees. Children
bend their knees and if hope is on
the lines they may go down. Women
throw their keys. Men hammer as they
please and if faith is on the pavement it may drown.
They show you a casket while mourner's
lament and say death's an inevitable groan.
But if the plot's two by eight you may as
well wait, because there is not enough
room for the stone.

You cry in that cold room then come out
for more while they say "Patience's
a virtue." Yet while you wait they grab what
is great and say "Where have you been?"
"We missed you."
What is raised up on land with windows of
sand, onlookers say "It's so pretty."
But it's just another room where the
dust eats the gloom and tomorrow
it's just one more city.

You thought you were starving while
someone was carving the Holiday
Turkey Breast. Though what they didn't
say when hell fell in your way. "You were
wise to mourn for the best."

So you're in a smoky room and everyone's
abloom and a lot of people pat you on
the back. But you fall down on your knees
and cry out to them please. "My soul, my soul!"
"I just want my soul." But it's not anywhere
among them in the pack. So the door with the exit
sign is open now and you run to it while you can
still see. What's on the other side no longer fascinates
your pride. Devils or Angels if they
will just let you be.

Blasphemy My Clothes

Because I read many words and saw blasphemy.
Blasphemy my heart.
Blasphemy my clothes.

Because I read so much into the words and
wanted to touch only your hand.

Yet sometimes I wanted to touch every part of you.

I wanted something.
A couple.

Numbers filled with blasphemy.
Me.

Didn't blasphemy cause most everything to do or be?

Hearts pounding on doors. Fists pounding.
Doors.

Oh so many doors!

Come drink with me blasphemy tea.

My heart -
My clothes -

Blasphemy

Me

No One's War

Suppose I said there was a war and
no one knew what it was for.
No one stated why they fought.
Or from what region they were brought.

For no sage or mystery or
no page in history.
Good, gentle men prepared to die.
For no apparent reason why.

Yet fight with guns, and knives and swords.
For no one and no awards.
One brought his rival's arm to him.
To mark a very foolish whim.

The soldier cried – most aloud.
Leave it with me for my shroud.
The other ran with shoeless feet -
over bloody, trampled meat.

He sang a song of victory.
Most aloud – no one to see.
Aghast at corpses all around -
he finds a rifle on the ground.

He holds it to his ringing ear.
Now the angels he can hear.
And horses ran without their men -
into nowhere – somewhere when.

Poem 68

The last scar on his body was branded by
love not lost or found.
The last mirror that showed his reflection
was released into the abyss.
Some declare that it's journey will
have no end.
He knows another outcome.
He believes he knows the Hand of love.
And the Sun.

A million suns. Are they not branded
by their explosions into darkness?

He knows darkness that he carries
like a lost brother.

A million brothers.
Are they not lost?
Yes, by explosions into darkness.

He carries questions and longing
for answers.

Questions mounted on his back.

And answers released turned
to rivers of his blood.

It's So Witty and Warm

It's so witty and warm there in the Spring. I am
going to go. Oh we've talked about so many
things, lately. About digging graves, cold rain
falling on naked skin. And how loneliness is like
getting married or walking in the sun. I hear Winter
there is like dust on the moon. Silent – Cold – Unmovable -
Strong. So I will bring plenty of clothing that
represents who I am – I am – I am.

Or I will run naked and allow icicles to hang off
my hair. Allow the sun to turn my nose a crimson
red. Ah, we've talked about many things. "Will this
end soon." "I don't want to hear it anymore."
"I care about you." "I'm really worried about him."
"Don't come in this house again." "Are you alright."
"You sound terrible." "Oh it's nothing. I've just
been screaming." "You know sound travels faster
under water." "They are going to hear."

Oh I am going to go for sure. I've traveled from one end
of the earth to the other end, in cold rain, mind you.
Then got back to that warm resting place in time to
sleep away the monotony of my journey. I awoke
as if nothing had ever happened. And later. Very
much later, we talked about much better things
turned out to be. I told you of a frightening dream
I had. Then you reminded me it was not a dream.

We laughed until we cried, as I recall. Oh
please tell me it will be warm there. Tell me dust
is Unmovable – Strong. Yes, strong like me.
We can talk again. I am going to go.
I am. I am. I am.

To My Garden

I could not bear a mistake nor a mistake bear me
so I was always writing and tearing.
I could only stand the sound of few voices
so I was always leaving and glaring.

What sticks? What stones do I feel? None I
say and bitterness for those who throw them – none.
Intellect wasted on ambition! Ambition wasted
on comfort and convenience! Comfort to rot the bones!
Convenience to finish them in the dust!

When did someone stop me in the hall of life
and proclaim "Love is worship clothed in desire
that biteth, biteth, biteth." Or better still. "Love
is nil worth looking for but will embrace one for
every turn around every corner when the
longing finds one happily silent and alone."

It's the silence that tears and smashes. Not for
its lack of beauty. For it is truly beautiful. But
because once silence is found wholly desirable
only real love and beauty can fill it up. Anything
else, breaks the spell. And Oh what a hot and hungry
spell love is! One may as well walk about with an
apple on their head for the arrows to come.
Or have two apple cores in their hands
to stop the bleeding.

Apples, apples, everywhere and not one pie to
stick my thumb in. So climb an apple tree boy
and don't come down. Eat and sleep in it. Don't
make a peep in it. Hide your face from those dark
branches when you choose. Play hide and seek, no
need to speak or gaze at anyone with the blues. If
anyone needs me they can shake it. If anyone wants
me they can chop it down.

No matter. My world is full of apple trees to
to find me on my apple knees.
I could not bear problems nor could problems
bear me. So I was always running and caring.
I could only stand the sound of your eyes so I
was always searching and staring.

What branches? What remorse for losing them
do I feel! None I say! And remorse for those who
would throw them in the fire – none!

"Love is an apple, clothed in beautiful apple skin."
I biteth, biteth, biteth, and quiteth the sin."

Printed in the United States
By Bookmasters